FACE
TO
FACE
WITH
GOD

To ~~Barb~~ Jo!
With fond memories
and much *Love*!

Betty

12/19/~~28~~

FACE
TO
FACE
WITH
GOD

From the Pen of a Modern Christian Mystic

BETTY W. SKINNER

To order additional copies of this book, contact:
Xlibris
1-888-795-4274
www.Xlibris.com
Orders@Xlibris.com
720695

CONTENTS

DEDICATION

This book is an offering of gratitude to God for the courage, the constancy, the creativity of those who walked the Way of Love before me. They are those whose spirit merged with mine, whose lives reminded me, again and again, of the Holy Image in which we are all framed – in Whose Great Love we are all loved as One.

Preface

At the beginning of all creativity is an inner vision in which what is to be created is experienced as complete. We see into the vision. It is a reflection of divine intentions as felt by the heart. The vision and the inspiration for the book you are holding comes from an infusion of Spirit as given to me over the decades from others who experienced divine intimacy.

Though chronological times and language often vary, the message is the same. The message is an ardent desire to touch the edges of God's Incarnate Word, knowing that such words coming from the intimacy of divine relationship are both loving and fruitful and speak from the heart into the hearts of others. Such words and thoughts are vital in an ever-deepening movement and dimension of Christ's teachings – the Way of Love.

This book is an attempt to move with the flow of a few given words from depth unto greater depth, to be alerted to the Truth that there is displacement, movement, growth, dying, death ever going on, like shadow waves of light, changing, exchanging in the lament of autumn's earth and air, colors burning, deepening, dying.

These gleanings are my ponderings. They are unlockings, leakings from a lifetime of longing and listening. They are revealed as I suffer the struggle to be freed of conditioning imposed by conventional wisdom and as I experience the awakening of an ever deepening Life in Christ. We are receptacles, instruments for all of life to flow through. We are asked to be humble, to be vulnerable and to learn from our failures.

We will never experience the vastness of our own inner truth until we dare to let go into the darkness. Paradoxically, it is in the pain of darkness that we begin to open towards the Light of Love. Though we make feeble attempts at expressing God's Love through writings, poetry, music and art, in its truest sense, Love cannot be said. Love can only be felt with the heart.

It is my fervent prayer that these gleanings will awaken within you the courage to change, to let go and to grow – that they will point you in the direction of the Unknown Whose Light, Life and Love will forever captivate your spirit and nourish your soul.

Hermitage   BWS
October 2006

ONE

Let There be Light

Recollection
Focused attention stilled in the present moment

Divine Purpose

Beyond the mist of egoic purpose lies an alternative purpose, a divine purpose, God's purpose for our lives.

We are tasked by some mysterious draw to elevate our lives through conscious endeavor into the high places of Spirit. We are asked to perfect, within the very core of our being, a supernal consciousness that transcends, then transforms the atmosphere through which we see and take breath. It is a consciousness that affects to the highest degree the quality of each moment, moment by moment. We are awakened to grasp the elusiveness of holy atmosphere and to thread it through with divine purpose, to paint for others streamers of Living Light and shimmering glimpses of Transparent Love. Beyond the mist we come to understand it is in dying that we awaken to divine purpose.

Purity

"The pure in heart, they shall see God."* Purity is given to us by the One Who sees us purely. God is the Pure One. He purifies us by gazing His purity into us. Our part is to stop, turn, open ourselves to receive His loving gaze. The pure person is one who has a vision of the whole, who sees all things in God, a vision that is without blinders, illusions and clutter. Impurity is partial vision. It is the false self's ability to separate that which should not be separated. God's purity is above our finite minds but not beyond His infinite will for us. He desires our purity, so pure the Light shines through. God waits, weeps in longing for us to return His loving gaze.

Longing

God is our destiny. We are His prayer, His thoughts. He is hopelessly lost in His Love and longing for us. When the spark of our own longing is set aglow by a glimpse of such unspeakable longing, we are drawn towards His Presence. As our longing intensifies, the Light brightens within us, thinning the veil. Our longing becomes our belonging – one with the longing of God.

Awareness

Awareness is the power that is hidden within the present moment. It is the power of God's Presence now. Once we awaken to such clarity of vision and focused attention, we're no longer distracted or pulled off course. Our ultimate purpose, as believers, is to glorify God by living our lives empowered by His Loving Presence, step by step, moment by moment. God does not want us to postpone to the future the joy of saying by our lives, "Now unto Him… be the glory both now and forever."

Accountability

We must be accountable to God, free of fear, and clear of inner clutter before we can hold another to the deepest truth and highest good. We inspire others by living sacrificially the beauty of our own poured out life. Thus the life of our own devotion to the Highest Good becomes a treasure for God in the hearts of others. All that enters our lives is a means of showing renewed devotion and love, a means by which we grow in courage and certitude. Only the highest good is a life compatible with God's Presence.

Plenitude

We cannot comprehend the abundance of God. Our egos do not allow room for such bounty. We are bound by the rules of conventional wisdom. Plenitude – God's vision for us – was lost in the lust for an apple. Yet the Gate never closed against us. God's plenitude assumed a body – the Christ – only to die on the cross and to regain entrance into God's vision for us.

Failure

Deeply rooted in our cultural conditioning is a false structure of values. It is a system that exalts quantity over quality and objects over personhood. We are conditioned to view failure as a dark experience that tells us we are inadequate. It is precisely this negative way that we choose to view our failures that activates and reactivates anxiety as well as shame.

In the eyes of the world, Jesus failed, too. Yet His vulnerability and humility show us the way of compassion and love. He asks us to embrace and learn from our failures. The water we once poured into the wine cannot be drained off, but mercifully, if consecrated, will be redeemed.

Darkness

Our tragic, endless search for security in exterior validation keeps us hostage. Our desperate clinging to convention gives an illusionary sense of control. Our fretful, frantic need for certainty becomes numb complacency. In the meantime, the Stranger remains a stranger.

Trust

Trust is the foundation of relationships – relationship with God, with self, and with others. Without trust there can be no safe place, no vulnerability, no intimacy. Each of these relationships lies withering and thirsting in the flatlands: no soulfood, no soulmates – our own soul is starving. Trust is an expression of the gift of ourselves in deepest gratitude for the gift of God's Unspeakable Love.

The Cross

The cross is the gateway to oneness with Infinity Itself. Yet we do not pass right through. We must stop and abide in the Life that we find there – the passion, the compassion of the Crucified. His is an anguishing so despairing that darkness pervaded the earth. It takes this same darkness and anguish to pierce, then to break our hearts. We seem to neglect the fact of suffering. The hope of our redemption lies in the overflowing of Divine Love pouring out of an unimaginable, immeasurable suffering.

Vulnerability

If we are ever to come face to face with God, we must first come face to face with the vulnerability of Christ's passion – a suffering Love made manifest outside the city gate – Golgotha. Vulnerability is the font of healing. To be renewed by such refreshing waters, we are asked to offer everything: a willingness to sink deep down into the muck and horror of that imageless nudity which is the Crucifix. To embrace the breathlessness of such agonizing affliction is also to embrace the unspeakable breathlessness of ecstasy. Within this paradox of extremes lies the mystery of Divine Vulnerability – a vulnerability so radical, so profound, as to silently absorb God's pain, our own pain and the pain of others. Here where Jesus Christ is stretched out, God turns toward the universe in forgiveness.

The Tomb

We move from Good Friday to Easter Sunday omitting Holy Saturday... the tomb. In a world that victimizes with all its lavish lures, the tomb, with its darkness, exists with little consideration. Solitude becomes a great struggle for those of us who would choose to be pure. In the silence we hear only the false voice of the ego and forget that true solitude, tomb time, is being with Christ in His darkness. Our Light-Life blazes out of a darkness shared with the Compassionate Christ.

Sacrifice

We were created out of sacrifice. God dared to risk His own image. In the beginning, we were free of self image. Our souls were aflame with the Light of Divine Love. Free will extinguished the Flame. Self glorification was the beginning of darkness. Yet God never leaves us wanting. We can choose to rekindle the flame. We are granted a chance to die, to offer our lives as living sacrifices. Whoever would enact such a sacrifice must renounce all self-image, as with Christ, must be hideously vulnerable, open and free to choose the will of the Father. Only then can our lives reflect the likeness of God.

Humility

Humility is the Way of Love. It is that lowliness of heart which seeks nothing for itself. It is an unselfconscious way of being. Humility is in constant conflict with pride. Pride is the false self's illusions and conclusions which promote an inordinate and blinding self-consciousness. The descending way of humility is a movement towards True Self's realization. By descending, we expose the false in order to perceive the true. The path of humility goes through humiliation. The endurance of insults and humiliation, inflicted on us by pride, have one indispensable condition: our consent to suffer the pain silently and alone for the sake of Love's Way. Gently yet painfully, our consent brings us to that low, empty place within where the Holy One and the human one meet - profound humility.

Mercy

Mercy is an intimate and inexhaustible energy generated within the relationship between the Father and the Son. It is the Light, the Life, the Spirit of Love. Its power is the transforming power of compassion that enters our pain and brokenness, healing all our wounded and bleeding places. Unlike grace, mercy is reciprocal. "Be merciful just as Your Father is merciful."* We are a covenant people. Our part, therefore, is to know God as merciful and to believe He understands mercifully. It is this holy reciprocity that opens us to embrace the whole wounded world, to see all things as one, mercied by the fathomless Love of God.

Compassion

Compassion is the Spirit of the Incarnate Christ knocking at our door, longing to enter into our confusion and pain. It is subjective, relational and deeply intimate. It is a suffering with, a fertile suffering. Pain embraced has purpose. When embraced in and with Christ, it begins to birth His Compassionate Life within us. For compassion is a life compatible with God's Presence and purpose. It is holding others in one thought at one time, at all times, in Love's great strength and passion.

Compassionate Co-suffering

Compassionate co-suffering possesses the Presence of redemptive Love. Self-obsessed co-dependence cannot coexist with compassionate co-suffering. The purity of Love's force pouring through the compassionate co-sufferer strips the self-obsessed co-dependent of the power to disturb. Focused attention frees the compassionate co-sufferer of all defensive, negative egoic involvement, thus bringing a silent stilling into the midst of the chaos. The chains of co-dependence cannot be broken until its lie is seen and confessed in the arms of Christ. It is within this mystery of compassionate co-suffering that reconciliation and healing are hidden. The tragic truth seldom grasped in the dysfunctional behavior of co-dependence is that both un-evolved participants are denied the honor of sharing in the passion of the Crucified Christ.

Divine Dignity

Love affirms and honors the dignity of each human soul. Love senses no power or superiority in the humiliation and desecration of another fellow sufferer. On the individual's part, we must never succumb to despair. It is beneath Love's affirmation and applause to consider ourselves beyond the reach of divine dignity. Each one of us is a precious piece in the great mosaic. Such dignity of soul requires obedience to a Higher Power, strength of Spirit. We are the beloved of God.

Harmony

To be fully alive in the world, to live and work with another within the compass of one heart, we must move to the side, must make ourselves as nothing, so that the other has space and does not feel threatened. Only those who have confronted their pride and have attained humility fully experience harmony in relationship with God, with others and with self. Such harmony opens an infinite vastness for others to move freely and breathe New Life.

Patience

Patience must first be seen as a spiritual discipline before it can be transformed into a holy virtue. Patience is Love waiting to begin. It asks for persistent practice and deepening awareness. It is Love waiting for us to do what we can in order to receive from Love the hope and encouragement to do what we cannot. As with all holy virtues, we must embrace the travail of our own inner transformation before we can see others with the eyes of Christ's own patient compassion. Infinite Patience brings us to that sacred place of belonging. Here, we are capable of embracing our own infirmities and brokenness as well as the infirmities and brokenness of others. Such Infinite Patience is Christ fully formed and being formed within us.

Words

We are inundated by a torrent of words that say nothing. They no longer communicate, foster communion or create community. We all live in them, think in them, feel in them yet have forgotten how to be still and dwell upon their dignity and power. Words are not given time to take root in the soil of our soul, not given time to utter fully the silent passions of our hearts. We have lost patience with solitude and silence, the home of The Word, thus leaving the depths of life untouched.

Christ is the Incarnate Word. His words are the language of God. They touch the heart and nourish the soul. Words held in the Divine Light of Love are infused by the Spirit of the Incarnate Word.

Listening

"Do you have ears and fail to hear?"* The kind of hearing that Jesus desires is free of fear and selectivity. It is a contemplative response that seeks to listen to the Voice of Love. The ears with which we hear the Voice of Love are hidden in the heart, and these ears do not hear clearly until they are free of static and favored with solitude and silence.

Learning to listen to the Voice of Love is a very demanding choice that requires discipline, awareness and patience. Yet as the static begins to clear in the stillness of solitude and silence, holy listening begins to clarify itself. We slowly begin to hear with the ears of our hearts. When we listen in and with the abiding Presence of Love, we are offering Love as well. Infinity Itself becomes the sound, the voice in each of our encounters with others. Love's Voice makes luminous the moment.

Wisdom

"Christ the power of God and the wisdom of God."* Christ not only leads the way to wisdom, but is the very flowering of wisdom within us. Wisdom does not exist in any outer teachings. This is second hand. Wisdom resides within us. It is the true self's own experience. It is first hand. This shift from our heads to our hearts, from having heard to beholding is what the Good News affirms. The wisdom of God is hiding in our hearts, beyond the veil of our illusions. Our task is to persist through the veil, to allow wisdom to emerge from the Truth of our own enlightened life.

Discernment

Discernment is one of the most important virtues of the spiritual life. It tells us what God wants of us and what He does not want. To discern God's will requires a blending of ingredients: knowing one's foundational identity as Christ's chosen, listening obedience to the inspirations of the Holy Spirit, and allowing God time to disclose impulsive, habitual reactions. These bring our choices to places of quiet, loving responses. In its essence, discernment is prayer. It composes a holy and compassionate life.

Gratitude

Gratitude is the giving and receiving of Love. Until we surrender and are awakened to the Light in this profound exchange, we are still in bondage. The movement from bondage to freedom is not complete until the Giver of Love becomes the Receiver of Love. The moment we actualize the gift of Love as ultimate gift and acknowledge our total dependence on the Giver, we are free. We are free to go forth into the fullness of gratitude – the Light that is the seed of Life and fills the circle of Love.

Truth

Truth cannot be known on the flatlands of the Spirit. To proclaim Truth through shaded illusions and intellectual synthesis is to deny Truth, its mysterious splendor and innermost essence. Truth is stingy in its offering; it protects itself against desecration. Truth is passionate; it is demanding. We must climb the mountain.

Holiness

Holiness, in its purest spiritual sense, means Truth. Holy Truth sees through the cloud of egoic experience and multiplicity. It sees things as they are. As we continue to abide in Holy Truth, the blindness of dualistic vision is healed. We wake up. Everything at every level is seen as connected, is seen in harmony and unity. All things become one in God. Those who attain to this state are called holy. They walk with Christ, and God is within reach of their hearts.

Hope

Resting in the shadows between faith and love is the illusive virtue hope. Hope is not the same thing as optimism. Optimism has a certain tension about it. It is not free because of our illusions and our unwillingness to accept things as they are. Hope, in its purist form, is perfect freedom perfected as we choose to accept in Love whatever God brings as good. Pure hope not only seeks God and the Way of Love to reach Him, but hopes always to experience God's Infinite Love both from within and from without. For those who deliberately choose to act only for the glory of God and the good of others, to eliminate all selfish and self-regarding motives from their lives and their work, hope becomes the gold cord in the landscape of their quest.

Yes

Yes is the answer to every why, and yet most of the time our yes is conditional, conditioned by the false self that is fearful of offering everything. It is to Christ we address our flaming yes. The yes of our hearts is our full response to the faithfulness at the heart of all things. In saying this yes, we release all our conditions and fears into the arms of Love, freeing us to become what we are. Our true self is yes.

Go

To most of us, go implies an outward movement - going, doing. However, in a deeper sense, go also implies an inner movement - being, abiding. To go in the name of Jesus requires a going in and a going out. The going in awakens us to our inner clutter in order that the going out can manifest the Light of Love. Finding such balance between our outer and inner life transforms and illuminates, drawing us into relationship with the Sacred. In the fullness of knowing, go no longer is a question of where to go or what to do, but rather how to live the manifestation of Divine Love, how to go from the cloistered seclusion of stillness and prayer into the mundane chaos that waits to engulf us.

Spiritual Model

When Jesus said to His beloved disciple, John, "Behold your Mother,"* He gave Mary to all of us. Somewhere in time and place, along the way of Love, we all meet Mary. She symbolizes in her body the essence of purity, innocence and simplicity. In her spirit, her unconditional yes to God's request was "I am the Lord's servant."* Her chosenness and submission happened in perfect fashion, so we can look to her as our model. She is one of us and she is what we all long to become – a mirror of Christ's perfection for others. Have you met your Mary yet?

Everything

A poor widow came and put in two copper coins which are worth a penny. Then He called His disciples and said to them, "Truly I tell you, this poor widow has put in more than all of those...for all of them have contributed out of their abundance, but she out of her poverty has put in everything."*

TWO

Let There be Life

Meditation
Each tiny particular illuminated by Love

Awakening

a perpetual succession
of refreshing clarity and Light.
Waking up to the wisdom of God.
Grasping the elusiveness of holy atmosphere.

"Let this mind be in you which was also in Christ Jesus."* Christ is the only consciousness that is fully awake. His is the possession and manifestation of Divine Light, Life and Love. Only the absolute purity of His Spirit can penetrate the blindness and self-enclosed darkness of our own spirit. Our finite, cluttered self -consciousness brings deep sorrow to the purity of Christ's selfless infinite consciousness. His compassion awakens us.

Mystery

awakening to Infinity,
a moment of Presence,
Love's passion.
Mist, mountains, rain drops,
a field of sunflowers,
the fragrance of a lily.

All of life flows in an intimate proximity to the sacred. It is this proximity that endows everything that exists with ultimate significance, with Supernal Beauty and Mystery. To feel within our very being this continuous rhythm, to live immersed in its sacred love flow, is to live in vibrant harmony with the Mystery of Life. Such an extraordinary awakening, such an intimate way of living is conversion. It is to know that the meaning of life is held in the wondrous Mystery of God's Love.

Beauty

a holy dimension,
an infinite shimmer.
Lifting the veil of the known,
peace flowing through a pure heart.

The persistent yearning that sweeps us all is a yearning to be known as we are and to be loved. When the wave of this yearning swells in our hearts and its crest is infused by wondrous Light, all our barriers are pushed aside. Beauty awakens within us. A momentous reality of God trembles through our veins, opening a glimpse of the Eternal. God answers with Love our trembling awe. Then comes a quiet wondering – how could we have lived in the shimmerings, the whispers, the intimations of such a Great Beauty and missed it? How could we be so blind?

Form and Fullness

clay in the hands of the Potter,
Spirit breathed into matter.
Entering into unity
through grace gaining
an unsuspected, transparent beauty.

We are creatures formed by God's hand and inspirited by God's very breath. It was God's boldest plan to predestine the merger of form and fullness (flesh and spirit). Living out this merger requires the reoccurring process of letting go and making space. We must be emptied then inspirited over and over again.

It is in the beauty of the Incarnate Christ that we behold the perfection of God's boldest plan: the merger of form and fullness.

Senses

sight, sound, scent, taste and touch,
outer soul sensors
opening into the world.
Intellect, memory and will,
inner soul sensors
opening into the heart.

The conscious and disciplined work of awakening our senses is vital to the Life of the Spirit within us. This work of awakening composes the movement from our heads to our hearts. Without such heightened sensitivity and purity, our outer and inner soul sensors remain starved. Starvation withers the soul thus denying us the experience of Presence. The marvel of the five senses - outer sensory aspects of the soul - is that we can experience the same world in five different ways. This is Creativity's gift, which when nourished, fuels our imagination. The imagination is infinitely and uniquely individual. It is our borderland, our dreamland between the outer and inner senses. The redeemed, transcendent imagination serves as a filter for our outer sensory experiences. It simplifies, clarifies, purifies, distilling our experience to its very essence as it enters the inner sensory aspects of the soul. As we choose to simplify, purify and intensify each sense, Love is freed to do what Love does: seeks, yearns, listens, draws, liberates, creates, recreates and, in time, manifests through us, a clear, pure Light – the Way of Love.

Conversion

holding fast the plow,
following the Christ,
entering into relationship.
Submission to the process,
open-ended waiting,
learning how to love.

We must choose to enter into our own recreative process; to be attentive to the Voice of Love and willing to embrace pain and suffering. Only in Christ is recreation possible. We are made to become what God has made. Our cooperation in this work is evidenced in the awareness of our own awakenings: moments of heightened perception, moving into the Beyond and close moments when we sense Another's Presence. It is in such moments that we are drawn into the Light of Love. To become one with Love, we must be born over and over again—conversion.

Faith

an earnest we hold,
a holy reciprocal.
The realization of Grace,
Ultimate Reality as gracious.
The soul's relevance
in accord with God.

Faith is a pilgrimage of the heart, a walk in the dark. It is an endless letting go towards the Light. Faith carries us along on a tide of God's promises beyond the mire and desolation of our own despair. It is God ringing our hearts like a bell, a holy summons asking us to take the next step into the unknowing.

Constancy

steadfast faithfulness
to the inner draw.
Dedication of the will
consecrated to the Way of Love.

The way of faithfulness to the constancy of certain spiritual disciplines amplifies and binds our intent to the intent of the Spirit. Though we oftentimes find it difficult to still our minds and enter into our hearts, constancy will slowly prepare the soul for the Spirit's entering. When constancy is offered in humility and simplicity, it is like spreading a beautiful quilt of wildflowers out before God, then patiently waiting to gather them in perfect harmony with God's purpose for our lives.

Holy Virtue

integrating
the three supreme virtues,
faith, hope and love,
into our Light-Life.
Filling our emptiness,
healing us.

Jesus can only speak from the hearts of those who have received Him. He speaks to us and from within us to the Father. We are not always conscious of Jesus keeping us in perfect oneness with the Father. Such intimate intercession flows out of the One who is Himself Holy Virtue. As we choose to let go into the unity and purity of such loving, intimate intercession, Holy Virtue seeps into the very fiber of our being, healing us.

Prayerfulness

*pouring the fullness of our inner life
towards God in gratefulness.
A bold craving
to live in the Light
of His Countenance.*

There is a difference between prayer and prayerfulness. Saying prayers when the heart is not awakened becomes repetitive, without feeling, one activity among many others. Prayerfulness is a knowing of the heart that transcends and transforms every activity. Prayerfulness is prayer without ceasing. There is only one response that can maintain us in unceasing prayer: gratitude. Gratefulness is prayerfulness. Gratitude is all we can offer in return for our awakening to the Great Mystery in which we live and move and have our being.

Silence

an indispensable discipline,
an undisturbed stillness,
a breathless quiet.
The pause between the words,
the eternal language of God.

Silence is the heart's certainty of the captivating Presence of the Divine. It is a breathless quiet in which the Ineffable within us communes with the Ineffable beyond us. But most exquisitely, it is the love-glow of a lifetime in which Spirit and horizon are silent together.

Timeless Mornings

yielding to the draw,
a daring stillness,
the hush of silence,
a vast emptiness,
an overwhelming Presence.

To feel the morning opening gently, to yield to the draw of its quiet, its freshness, is to know God in it, is to pray. Timeless mornings require desire, discipline and detachment. We must open attentively and slowly, allowing the Light to pour into us, listening in the silence for the whisperings of the Spirit. Such quiet times teach us to trust what we hear, thus slowing and knowing, the balance between prayer and service – service and prayer. We will never suffer from roaming about in the emptiness of time. We will suffer for the lack of it. These are moments when we come face to face with God.

The Cup

remembering and partaking
of His suffering.
Drinking one's own death,
longing only for the intimacy,
belonging only to the Mercy.

"Can you drink the cup that I am going to drink?"* The cup that
is poured out for us is synonymous with the cup we are called
to pour out for His sake. Each day the cup of our desire must
be held out empty, as empty as we are that day... each day, day
by day. The first yes, followed by many more suffering yeses,
the dregs must be consumed... His life to receive, to hold, and
to give back.

Affliction

the transforming power of suffering,
distress, despair, degradation
all at the same time.
The point of the nail piercing,
entering the Holy of Holies.

Over the infinity of space and time, the infinite Love of God comes to possess us. We can consent to receive or refuse. Surprisingly, this Love offering comes in the form of affliction, in the image of the nail. The high cost of consent intuits our refusal. Finite vision sees no purpose in pain.

Abiding

an elevated place,
fruit hewn out of suffering,
a grafted consciousness,
paradoxically, a perfected co-dependence.

Abiding is letting go into the burning orange of sunset, staying the long, dark night and, in God's time, awakening to the beauty of the dawn. "Abide in Me" is the divine imperative. Jesus not only sustains life, but is the origin and source of life as well. It is the painful cut that grafts. Sacrificial blood is the bond. The high cost of abiding binds the soul to the Sacred.

Our Belovedness

uniquely chosen,
exceedingly precious,
unconditionally loved.
Turning towards the Light,
opening to Life,
enfleshing the Love.

How else can God get our attention but through suffering and pain? Such extreme affliction goes beyond our finite reasoning and our control. At such moments of great despairing we touch upon a further and deeper inner connectedness. We seem to move to a place of knowing that the frailty of all suffering humanity is understood and cared for. We sense that our most grievous of sorrows are held in the Highest Good – the Supernal Good made manifest in Jesus. This Good bears the burdens of our sufferings and sorrows and illuminates within us the Truth of our own belovedness. The challenge now is how to actualize this quiet eminence of being and belonging: I am the beloved of God.

Holy Poverty

emptying of self,
choosing to be stripped,
impoverishment for Christ's sake.
Without identity or claim,
poor in spirit,
a unifying deprivation.

Emptiness is indispensable for the receiving of Holy Poverty. We must choose to give ourselves to the transforming Flame of the fire. We can always pretend, because of illusions and external imitations, that we are poor. But Holy Poverty is a gift. It must be received over and over again in the emptied chambers of our souls.

Obedience

listening,
absolute dependency,
undisturbed communion.
Alone in the darkness,
the Spirit of redemption,
the bond of union.

The beginning and the end of Christ's redemptive work is the Spirit of obedience. In the beginning is His absolute dependence on the will of His Father. "The Son can do nothing of Himself."* In the end is His total bond with the world and all of suffering humanity. It is to this He obediently and unconditionally offers Himself. "I have come that they may have life, and that they may have it more abundantly."* Divine obedience is lived out at the last supper, is accepted in Gethsemane, is accomplished on the cross and is perfected alone in the darkness of the tomb.

Waiting

expectant,
open-ended,
filled with hope.
A crossing point,
a setting free,
a certainty.

Beyond all things – personal problems, the multiplicity of temporal desires, even mountains, meadows and skies – there is a sublime expectation, a waiting for. It is a sense that something has already been given, that something within us has awakened, has begun. It is a longing to be set free from the many fears that imprison us and to move into the ultimate freedom of what lies beyond. Waiting is a form of patient, present moment living, a crossing point between God and man.

Discretion

silence – God's persistent language
visible in the heat of accusations.
Disentangling the world's contradictions,
potential for a greater good.

"Do You answer nothing?"* But Jesus kept silent. His confidence was in His Father's purpose for such accusations. They must be expressed. His silence enabled the potential for a greater good. His discretion brings the resolution of the trial to a far more profound and relevant level. Jesus is handed over to be crucified, but no one went away unashamed. Pilate washed his hands of the whole affair.

Lament

a melancholy
of joys and sorrows,
of beauty and of pain.
A longing that stifles the heart,
a passion for Perfection,
the Infinitude of God.

The unidentifiable feelings given and experienced in the lament are not experienced because something must be attained. On the contrary, they are experienced so that the soul will not give up its quest. Such whisperings and longings give us a homesickness for something we once possessed, then lost. It is a gentleness, a softness that draws us, that gives us courage to persevere, the possibility of the impossible, the great paradox of life refreshed in Christ.

Perseverance

a believing persistence,
endurance under affliction,
blind to the pain.
Trusting the ineffable,
an unwavering assurance,
the supreme effort towards Life.

We will not find what is lost in greed, in cravings, in instant gratification. They neglect a suffering Love and the burning heart. We are not asked to be excessive, but to be persistent. We are not asked to abandon life and leave the world. We are asked to persist in the world, to keep the spark within aflame, to suffer His Light to reflect in our face. Let not greed, cravings, lust rise like a barrier to our believing perseverance. Momentary contentment is but a shadow, not the Light.

Spiritual Writings

severe disciplines
etched in pain,
immersed in purity.
Burdened desire,
divine encounters,
eternally inspirational.

By virtue of the creative gifts entrusted and the continuous graces given, the person who would write, does write, embracing desire, discipline and discernment. Thus it is that the Spirit of God speaks through the writer's words while the many others listen knowingly in silence. This exchange becomes a spiritual dialogue that, otherwise, could not have been experienced.

Cloud of Witnesses

an unseen presence,
affirmation from beyond.
A divine assembly,
Power from on high.

We live in the presence of the unseen. To become aware of this truth, we must part company with words. We can know it only in the solitude and the silence. It is to experience, in the relentless perfection of holy work, the hope, the encouragement, the endurance of the great cloud of witnesses, the communion of the unseen body of Christ. It is to sense being surrounded by their presence, their prayer and intercession. It is to be empowered by power pouring forth from this divine assembly of which we, too, are an infinitesimal part.

Death

the Friend who welcomes us home,
Portal to fullness and endlessness.
The ultimate surrender to the Divine,
a final letting go into Mercy.

Death is intertwined with life and to embrace it without fear is to embrace all of life with a burning and infinite passion. We are born out of Love and will die into Love. The fullness of life and the endlessness of death are both a living Presence. Such fullness, such endlessness can only be experienced in the present moment as Spirit. Thus, eternal life is not a perpetual future, but rather a perpetual Presence. Death, so grasped by the heart, will not be distorted by false cravings for immortality. Life in and with the Divine is reciprocal giving and receiving. We return our life for the gift of Life.

Focused Attention

motivating and inspiring Love.
Unity – inner harmony.
Undisturbed mystical sleep.
Recollected in God.

The early religious referred to focused attention as recollection, an inner gathering of enlightened essence for meditation and contemplation. Focused attention is the means by which the power hidden in the present moment is released. Love's energy is a powerful force. When fully focused then released it affirms, enshrines and gives Life. Focused attention requires a disciplined will and a mind that is still. Surprisingly, at moments of such heightened attentiveness, we forget everything else. The ego is succumbed by the power of Love's force. The false voice is suddenly silent. We see each tiny particular swelling into the beauty of the whole. The soul feels and the heart knows, kindling a living Light that is never extinguished.

THREE

Let There be Love

Contemplation
Beyond time and place resting with Infinity

One Gaze

When death comes
I'll see into its tight held mystery,
way beyond the dark abyss.
Unafraid, I'll trace my way
through its howling void,
held by One Gaze,
fully focused, fully known.

As I enter my eightieth year, I feel a confidence in God I have never experienced before, perhaps from opening more and more to an ever-increasing quotient of Divine Light and Life. From this One Gaze I, yes, even I, manifest Divine Love.

How much strength and time I have left is uncertain, but I feel an urgency to offer this outpouring. I am deeply grateful for what has been given, patiently waiting and trusting for what is yet to come.

Wonder

Today
I walked in God's cathedral,
its stained glass windows framed
in leaves of shapeless wonder
and etched in brilliant tones
of red and greens, of gold and yellows,
then brought to life and set aglow
by streams of sunbeams
flowing from a clear blue sky.

I remember the first time I was lost, all lost, in wonder. I was empty of self and filled with such an awareness of creation's splendor that my feet never touched the earth I was walking on. I thought that my heart could not long endure such grandeur. I wished that creation could cry so its tears could mingle with mine, but its silence, its secrets remained hidden, unbroken. Not even tears could sustain that which made my heart so heavy with wonder. It was God's Love that would linger.

Dawn

The morning sun,
its power, its light
diffused by scattered clouds,
yet transparent in their freedom,
illuminate the darkness
in soft and gentle pinks.
Love's passion.

I feel an inconsolable home-sickness to roam the universe free of flesh, in Spirit, to saunter towards the Holy Land. Love's passion dawning every morning and I, weeping, as its light reached out and touched my heart. Love does that. Love reaches out; it weeps; it frees. Divine Love gives from its own experience and nothing in all of existence is ever turned away. The Holy Land, the realms of its enchantment transcended in the pink blush of the dawn—Love's passion.

Follow Me

From the depths of my being
my heart cries out:
help me to follow, Lord,
help me to follow.

Midst the pull of the world
be my center
that I might abide and be still.
Then help me to follow, Lord,
help me to follow.

He comes to me out of the mist and the rain on the wind, as One Unknown, a Stranger. His voice is in the splashing of the rain. His touch is in the moisture of the mist. He calls. He speaks, "Follow Me." To those of us who are obedient, He sets to the inner work of simplicity and clarity. In time, as if by some ineffable mystery, through our failures, conflicts, and sufferings, we come to know who He is.

Desire

Oh, the mystery of the Spirit's stirring,
the self erased and done,
my inner landscape ordered,
one of purity and truth.
A free and moving place,
abiding in communion,
a land I call desire, a land of yearnings,
a land where all my seasons meditate
and offer back their learnings.

Desire is what drew me to conclude that nothing would satisfy
my desire except Desire Itself. For Love seeks a love of its kind.
Desire called my soul into the depths of its own True Self. Here,
in this place of union, Love is perfected. All things are One.

Woundedness

You are a God
of intimate compassion
Whose Spirit is among us,
a wounded Love,
wide open to despair.
All pain finds refuge there.

I lived among the wounds, "the cat faces" of a few surviving long-leaf pines. By chipping the tree, it yielded its gum into small containers. There are people, too, whom God chips, then applies little containers. From time to time, He collects the gum in order to process the yield. How mysterious this industry of redemption, so beyond our finite understanding.

Horizons

The shadow lines stretched long and westward,
mountain upon mountain upon mountain.
My eye, the only moat in the endless beams
of grays and of blues and of greens.

We all need horizons, a place of horizontal gazing, to clarify earth and sky, earth and sea, as they touch each other, a span of wordless wonder, the endlessness of Eternal Love. Where I live now is surrounded by other buildings. The view through my windowpane is vertical. My body is too frail to walk the fields and meadows, the mountains and shores, but my memory of being there is focused and clear. Time ripens our memories and lengthens our horizons, bringing the frailty of aging to a place of rest and peace. For me, there will always be fields and meadows, mountains and shores – soul food, Spirit drawing me into the beyond of horizons.

Grass Roads

There is an emptiness
deep inside of me, a loss
this lovely autumn afternoon,
as though the sunset shadows
that surround me
embrace my shadow, too.

The sunlight was a tenderness of autumn orange. The grass road scarfed in ribbons of goldenrod and airy stalks of purple thistle. Green palmetto fans were fillers in this delicate shadow-like life of twilight dying. Amid it all, one scarlet, burning leaf as if Love had touched, transformed it with Her bleeding fingers, beyond which lay that distant land of lost laments.

Light

Past the dark night,
past the morning star,
past the sunrise,
in my hands, the Light of day.

Within Light, its rays and radiance, its fleeting, flickering shadows, lies Life – Life's clarity, its purpose, God's glory and His dream. For timeless times, I've gazed, bathed in Light's breathless beauty – mornings, midday, evenings – longing to cup such brilliance, to hold the fleeting still. I've opened to the Light to allow it time to remake my chaos, to clear my inner clutter, to illuminate my truth—an inner stillness before the wheel begins to turn again.

Spirit of Place

And anyone who comes
must travel inward silently
with thoughts of destination.
Death's preparation –
a place called Julian's Rock.

I was never prepared for the flood of emotions that always swept over me as I approached my spirit of place, a place I call Julian's Rock, high in the mountains. I was stirred to my very depths and tears often filled my eyes. This quiet, isolated place had become, for me, the very heart of re-creative beauty, a place of transcendent joy, the joy of being, a place of awakened consciousness, the joy of abiding. My spirit of place became one with the Spirit of Presence. But what was most extraordinary, as I returned year after year, was what began to pour through me into the world: divine creative and re-creative words and works that offered its essence to others and changed their lives forever.

The Last Leaf

The green has turned to golden
some branches bare
their leaves have fallen.
And I, His chosen,
come again to ponder,
within the changing pattern
of creation,
the beauty in the dying,
the forgiving Face of God.

The beauty and freedom of remembering that flows out of gratitude is the gift of letting go. I remember the last leaf floating in the radiance of blue autumn sky leaving its branch stripped and exposed. There was no hint of despair or fear – only a rich and painless farewell for the gift of a passing season. The inner life of the branch seemed to quietly retire deep into its roots for renewal – to rest, to wait, to sleep. Once again, I was drawn into the truth of change and exchange, movement, growth, and dying. I was floated on the last leaf's moment.

Grace

How do I describe You, Lord,
as if I really could?
This ordination by Your Spirit,
this majestic encounter
of Your unveiling
in the silent dark
of contemplation.
How do I describe You, Lord,
as if I really could?

How could I dare be so presumptuous as to reduce Grace to words? Words would be an insult to the Eternal Giver. Grace is a gift. I am not free to demand it, but I am free to refuse it. Grace cannot be said. It can only be heard, branded, breathed. I must hear such Love in His words, "It is finished." I must bear such Love etched in the sufferings and hopes of my heart. I must feel such Love breathing a new Spirit into the depths of my soul, drawing me into the intimacy of His Own Life, changing my life forever.

Aging

Things are as they are.
The Love, the joy, the peace
to which I so aspire,
borne through Spirit, are mine, live on
only in what remains behind: my suffering.

Let me begin at the end. The diminishment and pain of aging have brought me to this place. It is no longer a matter of how to continue, but rather how to endure, how to finish well, how to return something beautiful to a bountiful God. I have come to know through the decades that the essence of Christian spirituality does not lie in entertaining a concept of God, but rather lies in articulating a memory of moments illuminated by God's Love and His Presence. Fragile, frail and mortal as I am, I look back with memories consumed by such moments of Presence and Love. Though the shadows are lengthening and the candle is flickering, soon to be snuffed by the unwinding of time, I wait and rest in thoughts that are compatible with my destiny. I see my life as a witness, my spirit echoing through all of eternity.

FOUR

Let There be Prayer

Transcendent
A conversation of Spirit

Blessed Love

Blessed Love, encompass me.
Pour Yourself over me.
Love, lift me up and make me whole.

Then, dear Love,
break me into a thousand pieces
and scatter me to Your Glory
that others might know Love, too.

And Love,
never even once let me ask
why or how or when
or fail to stand because of pain.
For You, sweet Love,
must not have died in vain.

Joy

Help me to remember, Father,
that this time of joy
will never come again.
Let me saver the fullness of it.
Let me share the beauty of it.
That others might feel
and know it, too.

Drawn

Dear God,
I am drawn into prayer.
The reality of Your Presence
is everywhere.
Fill my hurting, aching heart
with Your cleansing,
constructive, healing art.

Boundless Love

Oh, precious Jesus,
stay with me today.
Caress me in Your warming way.
Identify me with those above.
Fill me with Your boundless Love.

Forgiveness

Dearest Father,
in the quietness of this lovely place,
I feel Your Presence near.
I ask for Your forgiveness
to fill and free me from all fear,
to lift me ever upward,
to make me Your very own,
then use me for Your purpose
until I, at last, come home.

Christening Prayer

Precious Lord,
we who are so blessed, thank You
for the joy of this celebration,
for the welcoming, for the nurturing
of these two special children
into Your Holy Family.
May we as parents,
grandparents, Godparents
so live in Your Light and by Your Light
that our lives might illuminate theirs.

Grief

Liberate me, free me,
lift and hold me, Oh Holy Spirit.
I offer You my heavy, hurting, aching heart.
My grief is like a valley deep
with dark caves in which I hide.
My tears blur all my vision;
my pathway goes in circles,
each circle filled with pain.
There seems no map for sorrow.
And, Lord, I've lost sight of my tomorrow!

"Hold fast, my dear disciple.
Love claimed you long ago.
Your grieving is My squeezing,
the pressure of My hand,
a touch that knows your sorrow,
a touch that heals today,
that seals, reveals tomorrow."

Prayer of Preparation

Center me down, Lord,
to the innermost of my innermost,
until all of me kneels before You.
Then, in this night
as I sleep in Your Presence,
in the morning
as I awake in Your Presence,
silently, reverently, waitfully,
bring me to Your table
that I might
see with Your eyes,
hear with Your ears,
love with Your Love.

Beloved of My Soul

O, Beloved of my soul
yet again I come alone
to seek Your Face,
to hear Your Voice,
to know Your Heart
in quiet summer days,
in endless mountain ways.

O, Beloved of my soul
It's you I so desire.
Refresh, renew, refill me.
From morning mist
That lifts to pure blue sky,
Then hides You, Your mysteries,
In the silence of the clouds.

O, Beloved of my soul
from evening rapture, pink shadows
on the mountain face,
lost in the lingering of twilight.
It's You, Lord, Your Presence,
Your way of saying good night.

Lovely Maria

Lovely Maria,
Mother of God, you who
first identified with holy dying,
first participated in holy pain,
first beheld the Infant Face of glory,
God Incarnate.
Fervent lover of the Infinite,
teach me such intimacy
with the Beloved.

A Prayer for Simplicity

Most generous God, You gave me
memory, understanding and will.
You gave me memory
that I might hold Your blessings.
You gave me understanding
that I might know Your truths.
You gave me will
that I might love
what my memory holds
and my understanding knows.
Take my memory that it may no longer
be filled with thoughts of me.
Take my understanding that it may no longer
cling to so much that is not of You.
Take my will that it may choose
always to remember You,
always to see You,
always to love You.

Jesus, Precious Shepherd

Oh, Jesus, Precious Shepherd
what will You say to me
this Christmas?
What have You prepared for me
at Your nativity?

Will the noise of temporal things
silence the Heavenly Hosts,
the angelic song of praise
the Infant cry of glory
that bids me come,
that longs to claim me,
to rename me
Chosen, Blessed, Beloved?

Will the clutter,
the glitter of the world, blind me?
Will I fail to find You
in lowliness in the crib,
You, Holy Child of God,
You, His Gift of unending birth,
of everlasting beginning,
of joy, of peace on earth?

Oh, Jesus Precious Shepherd,
this Christmas,
help me to find You,
enable me to hear You,
give me Your Gift.
Be born anew each instant
in the manger of my heart.

Gentle First Truth

Oh God, gentle first Truth,
move in my heart.
Illuminate each dark corner
where webs of self still hide.
Show me Whose I am
that I might know who I am.
Then recreate me,
dress me in Yourself
whose virtue is love,
whose knowledge is truth,
whose beauty is creation.

Oh God, eternal first Truth,
You who created me in love
and longs to recreate me in mercy.
Bring me to the foot of the cross,
to the nailed feet, the gift of Your Son.
And there, in His shadow,
in unspeakable gratitude,
enable me to live consistently
the endless dynamic
of knowledge and love
of gentle first Truth.

Merciful Creator

Oh, merciful Creator
You, Totally Objective
and Transcendent,
where are You?
My spirit is in ruins.
My soul is in need.
I am barren, dry and empty.
Show me Your Face.
Offer me Your embrace.
Bring me to that quiet place
in the Beloved.

Oh, merciful Redeemer
You, Wholly Subjective
and Immanent, integrate me.
Nourish me in the Trinity.
Immerse me in the flow
of divine relationship.
Free me to live this energy,
this Spirit of Love,
and to accept all that it offers me
of light and darkness,
of life and death,
of agony and ecstasy.

Caught Between the Nails

Oh, Good Jesus,
hear me, hold me, love me
in this, the season of
my spirit's loss and grieving,
in the anguish of my waiting,
in the silence of familiar voices gone,
in the pain of all the change,
in the twilight of my years
before Perfection dawns
and I am gone.

Oh, Good Jesus,
I try the letting go,
to understand my weakness,
to trust You in my darkness,
to make room for Your grace to heal.
Yet there is no return,
only the echo of my own crying.
It seems I, too, with You,
am caught between the nails.

Oh, Good Jesus,
in this holy place of crucifixion,
broaden the boundaries of my heart.
Soften the hard places that
defend, define and deny.
Teach my heart to love.
Make it a refuge for others
who, too, are caught
between the nails.

A Prayer of Gratitude

Father and Author of Love
dwelling deep within my heart
together with Your Son,
shower Your compassion
on the frailty of my humanity.

Lift me up when I fall.
Forgive me when I fail.
Encourage me when I falter.
Perfect my ingratitude
that I might know You in Your Son,
that I might praise You, Father, with Him
and truly know Your gratitude.

In the sacrifice of the Eucharist
allow me the taste of New Wine,
to rejoice always in the experience
that You, Oh God, are Love.

Allow me the sight of new eyes
that I might recognize
Your Love in everything.
For in Your unfathomable generosity
You have given me everything.

May I take nothing for granted
and be constantly awakened
to new wonders, to new ways
of gratitude for Your goodness,
Oh Holy Father. Amen.

Illumination From Julian

O Trinity, my Eternal Lover,
O Passion, my Suffering Lover,
O Compassion, my Wounded Lover.

Grieving that I have forgotten You,
mourning that I do not draw near to You,
weeping that I am obsessed
with muchness and manyness.

Heal the blindness of my heart.
Open unto me my Hidden Center.
Unravel the mystery of this inner space,
the sweet, sweet intimacy of our meeting place.

Please make Your Love known to me.
Free me from fear, anger and anxiety,
the pain of being human.
Enable me to embrace You,
and through You,
my deepest self as well.

Grasp of Love

Lord,
I sense a lingering lament.
That crushing grasp of Love,
my weary eyes are flushed with tears,
my ears discern a distant weeping,
a loneliness beyond all reason,
a separateness on earth, a search.

Lord,
so much of You is lost
in the shapelessness of clutter,
the false contours of life,
its sharp edges and illusions,
its starkness and its shimmering cold.

Lord,
grant new birth within my frigid sleep,
intensify my desire and my adoring,
a knowing beyond knowing,
that underneath each trembling edge
lies One Sweet Forgotten Secret:
the Gift of Love, a Child,
the Christ, a Savior.

Obscurity

I pray each day
the ever greater opening up,
to breath my native air,
to offer less of me to You.

Each day to hear
the silence of eternity
interpreted by Love.
By Your great Draw to be
completely hidden and obscure,
diminished, whatever the cost to me.

That my whole offering
is just an emptiness
for You to fill or not
according to Your will.

My Yesterdays

O Love, where are all my yesterdays?
I often rest in wonder.
Could all my yesterdays be caught
between my finite eyes?
The mountain...mine,
the meadow...mine,
the forest and its daybreak sky,
the whisper of the wind-touched leaves,
the freedom of the dipping bird,
the gold dust of the stars,
all mine to look at when I pleased.
Such news would break my heart
with praise, such beauty, blind my gaze.
O Love, where are all my yesterdays?

Moment by Moment

Oh, Love
Moment by moment my spirit runs to You.
Will You embrace and welcome me?
My longing heart waits Your reply.
Please, Love, look graciously.

I'll bring You rainbows and sunsets
and a gentle mist from mountain tops,
from Julian's rock,
from dancing brooks and quiet nooks,
from steadfast days in fertile lands
where no other reaper stands but You.

Oh, Love
if such beauty extinguish me,
if I gain Your Spirit free,
if death, its agony, its ecstasy
bloom my eternity, it's then I'll know
I've nothing left to bring.
For sun just touched the morning
and all my life is spring.
Moment by moment, Beloved, I'm Yours.

Beloved

Beloved,
embrace me
in the dark night of my praying,
in the deep silence of my offering,
in the confrontation of my dying.

Beloved,
enable me
by faith to know You without seeing You,
by hope to possess You
without feeling Your Presence,
by love to desire You above all desires.

Beloved,
grant that I might put
all faith in love for You,
all hope in love for You,
to know that all desires fail but one:
my desire to be loved by You.

Dear Redeemer

Jesus,
my Beloved, it's spring again.
I am Your prisoner, captured
in its sweet song,
in its warmth and fragrance,
in all the Beauty new life brings.
Waves of infinite tenderness
wash over me and all of Creation.
Your Divine Look
has penetrated my heart.
You only do I see.
It is my soul itself I offer Thee.

Dear Redeemer,
I long to gather the blooms
from each lovely flower
and scatter their petals in the dew
at the feet of Your Calvary.
I would so like to reach up
and dry Your tears.
Please know my sighs, my sorrows,
my joys, my little sacrifices
given in flames of love.
These are my spring flowers,
my petals in the dew.

Infinite Life

O God,
tenderest Love within my breast,
burning and Majestic Holiness,
in whom all Life freely lives itself,
Life that in me now has rest.

O God,
with wide embracing Love,
Your Spirit animates my fading years.
I see Eternity's brilliance shine
and Christ shines equal,
liberating me from fear.

O God,
You, the Giver, are Gift, Being, Breath.
In You there is no room for death.
Vain are the many worthless words
that move my lips but not my heart.

O God,
every existence exists in You.
I hold fast to Your Infinity,
submitting, not knowing to what,
crying, not knowing why,
entering, not knowing when.

Notes

Index

The Hidden Life, a spiritual autobiography (Kitty Crenshaw and Catherine Snapp, Ph.D., NavPress, 2006). Also in Spanish, by Christian Editing, 2012. Because of the book's efficacy in helping people suffering depression, it is used in the treatment plans at the Family Practice Residency Program at Tallahassee Memorial Hospital in Florida. A second edition is underway. Dr. Gerald G. May's endorsement: "This book is a work of love, revealing the many facets of this remarkable woman: her life story, her insights, and guidance, and her beautiful poetry. She will touch your heart in profound and healing ways."

The Circle of Love (Tumbleweeds Productions, 2006), embodies Betty's collection of poems, spanning six decades.

"Face to Face" and "Circle of Love" CD's are recordings of Betty reading her poetry, accompanied by concert pianist, Dana Cunningham.

Betty's work would not have reached the world were it not for the gifts of Becky B. Andersen, scribe and dear friend of over thirty years. Betty says of her soul friend, "I have never met anyone as close to God as my dear friend, Becky. Nor has God given me a friendship like ours that has grown into such a depth of love, trust, and faithfulness. Becky always pointed to God first, and everything she did she did with nothing expected in return."

Please send correspondence to Betsy
Skinner at 29thplace@gmail.com.

www.bwsministries.com

Book cover photograph by Dave Allen/Shutterstock.com

Printed in the United States
By Bookmasters